Whiskers of a Kitten

Whiskers of a Kitten

Kitty Lever

Louria Books

Published by Louria Books.

For information, contact catalog@louriabooks.com.

Trade Paperback: 979-8-90116-078-7

eBook: 979-8-90116-079-4

Library of Congress Control Number: 2026946807

Cover design by Ian Delucca

Louria Books
www.louriabooks.com

Imprimé au Canada
1 3 5 7 9 10 8 6 4 2

dear reader,

welcome. this is a collection of intimate thoughts and scenes from my life.

this is my catharsis.

these are confessions, secrets, moments of yearning, triumph, but most of all, it is an expression of honesty.

it is one of heartbreak, grit, love, the journey from oneself, and then coming home.

until i was sober, i always hated going home. maybe because i've never quite known where it was. i've always found a home in words. giving a feeling a body, naming it.

after my first heartbreak in new york city, a stylist i was working for said to me, "don't let the heartbreak just sit there, channel it, make the pain worth it."

this is for a 23-year-old version of myself, whose tears hit the pavement and wished on *one day*.

this is for sensitive souls who are told they are "too much."

* this is for those who talk to the moon.

this is for those no longer with us.

and for you, reader. thank you.

dear reader,

thank you.

thank you for being here.

p.s. to my parents who will read this, there are pages about sex, alcohol, and drug use. i know i am your daughter, but i am first just a human. a silly little curious human. just like you. my favorite people in the world, I love you. thank you.

Love,
Katie Lever

whiskers: extra sensory devices, a type of stiff hair used by mammals to sense their environment

did you Know whiskers can detect even the slightest vibration in the air?

you will be:

the hero, the villain, the damsel, the whore, the princess, the one that got away, the liar, the bystander, the savior, the clown, the wolf, the lamb

you will be flawed

and

you will be perfect

if you start this life clear as
water,

if you do it right,
you'll be mud

glittery, [illegible]
beautiful

gleaming black matter
a translucent film along the top
and questionably deep

you will never be as pure as you once were

and that is the whole point

i crave
the comfort
of a home

but not
the tension
of a house

CORDEIRO
2026

I'm a freedom girl
Reborn
Stuck in a video game

Still peeling moving stickers off the furniture
Still recovering from yesterday

Grew wings
Lost roots
my feet have never touched the ground

My curiosity is a revolver
Six ways to die
in my pocket

Heart in my fist
naked
pulling the trigger

The porch
where my shoes are too
small

The window pane
where I meet myself

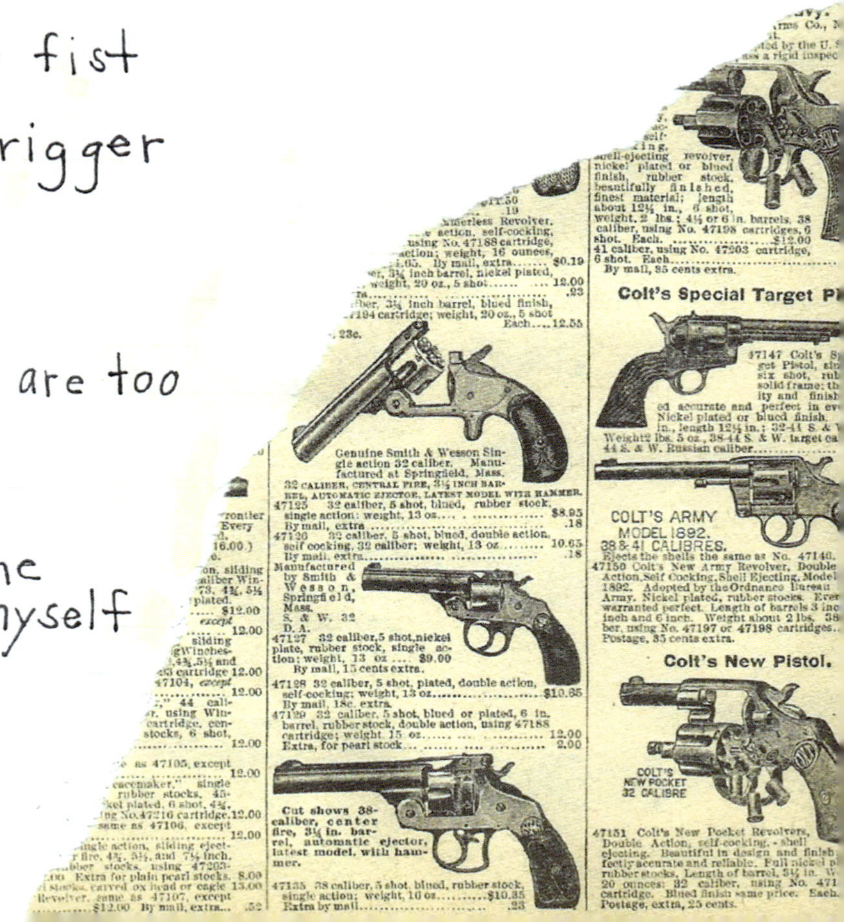

The streets
Where the dead soldiers are named

The door
where I wait for dad to come home

I am the dandelion you made a wish on
A gust
and I'm thrashing

Taps on a glass jar
Now you see me

Like a fire fly

Now you don't.

I'm drunk

on words dressed in nonchalance
"You don't kiss your friends?"

lips pursed in a question mark
Tongue loose,
drawling the line

you fuck me with my clothes on
I say, "that's hot"
being inside of me
without ever seeing me

The unspeakable avoidance
of being
freshly fucked
and
just friends

The audacity of my naked body
your tired warning,

"Baby, don't fall in love with me"

You turn with the words
so you don't have to watch them land

"Never that"
I laugh
count sheep

Paralyzed
dreaming
of
You
and
Leaving
before you could open your eyes

collected
like a doll
and not
a person
MONTGOMERY WARD & CO.'S CATALOGUE No. 56.
230
Kid Body Dolls, Ne Plus Ultra Patent Joints, Closing Eyes.
Dressed Dolls, Cloth Bodies, with Kid Joints.
Columbus Dolls.
Indestructible Wool Dolls.
Dressed Dolls, Patent Indestructible Heads.
Jointed Dolls, Dressed.
Clapping Figure
Dressed Dolls, American Bisque Heads.

i will be in heaven telling
god you didnt mean to

Red always telling on my [redacted]

Fair skin,
flushed
Two spades
Lust

in the back seat kicking
Red light
Red lip
Red
Red
Red

You wanted me on the wall so I begge
for the bed

Morning
embers
gutted carcass in the orange
Do you even know my name?
yellow gleaming horror

Green
I saw you
Soft
I saw me
Watch
I saw her
Blue

the night bleeds like a purple sky
Bruised

I am moonlight

lost

in these watercolor rendezvous

*** Food ***

#84 10:44 AM

Server: Morghan C

Tab:

1 I

…asted

For Here

Everything

…lain CC

Knife With It

1 morning

grieved

to go

sweet

expired

Knife with it

Stray kitten

alley cat
so mean and so soft

i once heard a story about a kitten
only dying

when someone tried to save it

worms in my belly
untreatable
unkillable

and i'll live nine lives

oops I said I

all the birthdays
i remember are
people im
trying to forget

CORDEIRO
2026

glittery green eye shadow
black liner
lacing up a platform boot to chase freedom

pink powder
tiny skirts

sceney
trashy
coy
ravenous

angels and their vices
wiping their nose with a
"nice to meet you"

it fills me up
it bottoms me out

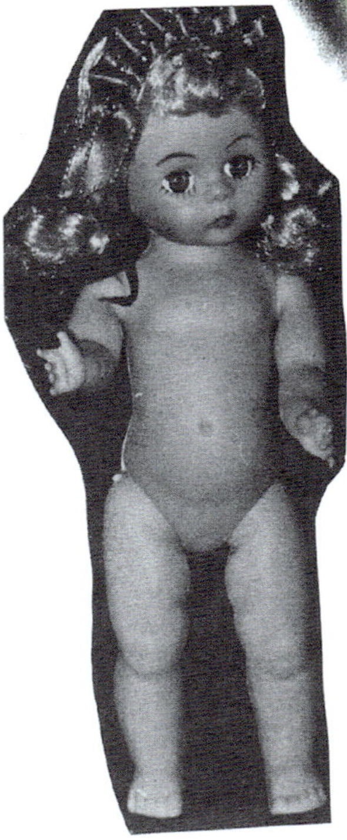

Strangers
8 a.m. in the bathroom mirror
"*how did I get here?*"

the subway
where the night rolled into morning

A girl
with bloodshot blue eyes
ripped tights her albatross
still high
fidgeting
riding the ride

I watch her
count the stops
nowhere left to hide

my name is
ynk and
iss you
my name is
do you remember me?
Hello
my name is
"not what we're looking for"
urs.
hine doll
Hello
my name is
manic pixie dream girl and i am here to save you (was that my line?)
Hello
my name is
luck
Hello
my name is
fuck yo
stargirl.
Hello
my name is
anger
Hello
my name is
fuck me

Band aid sex
the parking lot

a conversation of thrusts
our bare bones

the 13th minute interrupted by

I dread it

Your broken moan

hits me like a sunrise
coming to *and time to go home*

I savor the seconds
mourn your black eyes
kiss my teeth
Ponder another high

The void chirps
Innocuous nuisance

Stones like lines
Stones like climaxes
Stones like regret

I swallow them all
and bury the bird with it

~~Prized~~

Prized ponies on concrete
Fractured angel wings
Lined up
dressed for the slaughter

Wide eyed
from nowhere
performing for the pulsating void

"Point to the wound"

a nameless you

Amorphous beast
Are you a child?
a man?

the steps to the stage calling
me
up
next

Swallowed sobs
an auditorium of ghosts

I know why
the show girl weeps

You know the story of Alice right?
Alice moves to the city
The first time Alice feels pretty

Oklahoma, North Carolina, one of the two
A long way from home
The chance to be someone *new*

A tale as old as time
The desire to be desired
Oh, how addicting it is to be admired!

It's the nightlife circuit
It's deceit and demise
It's traveling the world on a billionaire's dime

A world of blacked out riddles
Tea parties and dares
A gamble with your life and dissociative stares

It's Hollywood in the flesh
A spoon to the nose
The intoxication that comes with finally being chose

It’s tonight!
At a round table,
With beauty so hypnotic,
Who knew innocence could be so erotic?

Ally sits next to Alice,
Ally that’s brand new
From Oklahoma, North Carolina, one of the two
“I moved here to model, how about you?”

“Oh, uh I model too”
It’s the first time Alice notices such young eyes
How long had she been in Wonderland unrealized?

“Alice, Ally, come on we’re running late!”

Down the rabbit hole to a similar fate

POST CARD

you are a beautiful girl
and they will call it a
silver spoon but it is a
Knife

[redacted]
THE [redacted]GATE AND THE KEEP
[redacted]

pendulum of wisdom

some truths, secrets, thoughts you don't say out loud but *here* you do

1. his texts should not make me this wet
2. I don't think I'm scared of death
3. But I found myself praying I don't die before Wednesday
4. It's Friday
5. *Nights*, when fate is delt in bathroom stalls
6. I've had sex in a bathroom stall
7. I've *saved* girls in bathroom stalls
8. I was one floor down when it happened
9. I wish I could've saved you too
10. *Did you know if an ambulance rescues an unconciou woman and the paramedics are two men, a woman has to accompany her?*
11. That was the first time I rode in an ambulance
12. She doesn't know I exist because I didn't stay for her to wake up
13. *I can't sleep*
14. Angels are getting their wings clipped in the middle of the night

Where was I?
Where was I?
Where was I?
Where was I?
Where was I?
Where was I?
Where was I?
Where was I?
Where was I?
Where was I?
Where was I?
Where was I?
Where was I?
Where was I?
Where was I?
Where was I?
Where was I?

I'm *running*
so I don't remember the dream
so I don't ache for my mom
to speed up
til my lungs burn
to feel closer to my dad
breathing
until I remember me
to forget you
or
blame it on you
no one can catch me
I'm racing the dogs
Faster
Faster
Faster

Because my dog is dead

And I haven't grieved him because I've been
Running
faster
Get Out
of
my head
How long
is *too long*?
How far
will I have gone
Until it's all gone
out of time
On the edge of the Earth
ready to fly
When will I grow wings?
When will it be my time?
Not yet
Please
I am so
Scared
to *die*
savoring the air
on my tear stricken face
Is there a sky
in heaven?
Do I have legs
in heaven?
Please God
I promise
to keep feeling everything
until it hurts
just keep me
for another sunrise

And please,

Take care of my dog

"Nothing lasts forever"
[clever ways to say goodbye]

Guest Check

Date	Table	Guests	Server	5142958

APPT - SOUP/SAL - ENTREE - VEG/POT - DESSERT - BEV

the ask me why
i go back

i tell them,
"have you ever been to
church?"

it goes sin
salvation,
fuck me,
no, fuck me

Tax

fuck me Total

on my Knees

EP3632-1

Guest Receipt

Date	Amount	Guests	Server	5142958
ForgixE mE				

Thank You!

1		love
2		is
3		disgusting
4		when
5		you're
6		begging
7		for
8		it
9		
10		
11		
12		
13		
14		
15		
16		
17		

Transfer to front Total

INSANITY

i know better
i know better
i know better
i know better
i know better
i know better
i know better
i know better

Who puts
a dead bird
in a gilded
cage?

i don't know
the void,
but i know
its shape

A leap down the rabbit hole
a story to tell
and

You

intoxicated, laughing
cheekbones dancing violently
Red light

green
and I blink
sending a prayer to God

Can you make me gravity?

I'm stuffing time in my pocket, seconds too
closed fists
a wolf's smile

When does a fawn begin to smell?

Eyes filled with apology
Mouth open hanging on a sorry
Sorry

Stuck in a reflection
Chasing

Chasing, chasing, chasing

Grass stains
Galaxies
Surrounded by my own scent

God, Can you at least make me angry?

the only thing that saved the Mad Hatter from darkness was whimsy.

indulge in it.

leg cramping through an orgasm

Innocence
depravity
a tiny pink bow

he likes the way I talk
in riddles

The way I
flit my Bambi eyes

Porcelain
rotten
Kind

"You're like a magic 8 ball, I don't know
what will come out of you next"

I ash an unlit cigarette on my antique lace

I think I'll die with a smile on my face

they found me in the backyard
digging up a grave

the melody of nostalgia
brought me
to
my
knees

your stolen laugh

lures me to the water

Tall grass
chiggers biting at my legs

I'm running with dirt in my fingernails [redacted]
searching for your face

CONSTANTLY
PICKING
AT
SCABS

You want to be poeticized
but you don't want to be perceived

You want to fall in love
but you can't stay still

and when you want to stay,
You'll leave.

Open casket going 6 feet under
You must be so proud!

Hero of the grey
eyes as big as the moon

You're still the same
Scared
little

Girl

Mo | Tu | We | Th | Fr | Sa | Su

Memo No. ______
Date / /

Should I call you God?

Fo r birthing the words that
sh attered
my
knees?

bloody Knees

sinking

deeper

i pray to the
unnamed
saint
of
your
holy
silence

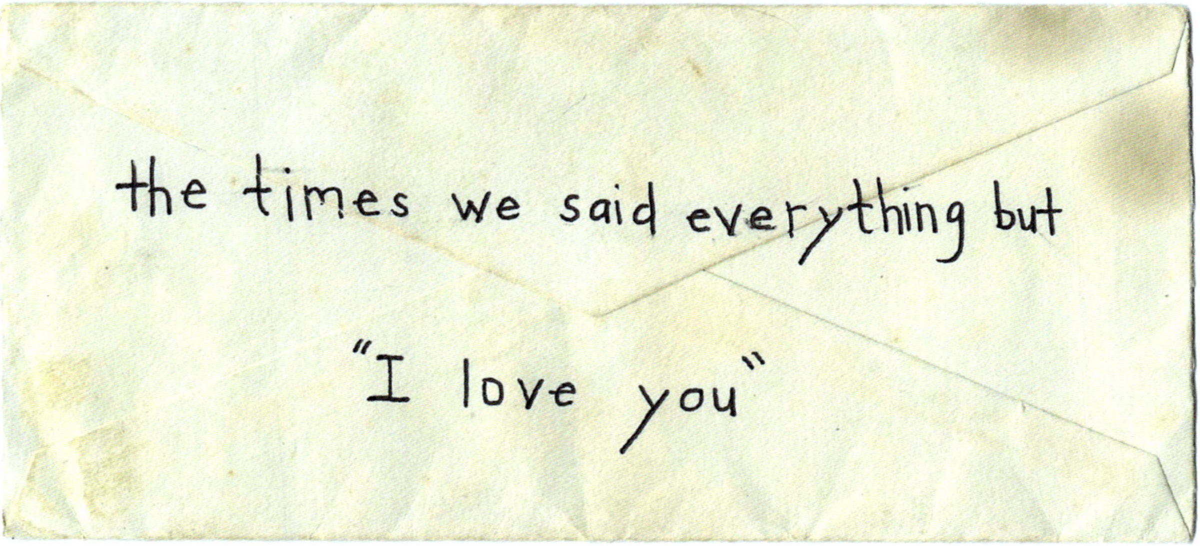
the times we said everything but
"I love you"

"I'm a victim!" I tell the butcher

I lie naked on the table,
place the Knife in his hand

"Are you going to hurt me?"

I beg for it

My pupils dilate

Brace for pain

I moan instead of scream

watching myself
watching you
watching me
grief
because you adore me
i'm listening to lightening strike
and you think about me
thunder roll
but never in the way i wish we could be

cause
and i adore you
and effect
i think of you too
i just wish things could be different
i sit here paralyzed
but i'm scared
“sorry”
waiting for you to make a move
like when i asked you for permission
hot glass
because you adore me, yes
against my skin
you think of me too
like a supernormal stimulus
like Hathos
but the way i want you feels like i can't move
compulsion of revulsion
and even when i try to run
“sorry”
like a pleasurable sense of loathing
what moves my legs is you
like something in my hands
but i could never hold it
i'm listening to lightning strike
like hot glass right out of the kiln
a sharp hiss
and the mirrors
the fucking mirrors
you're surrounding me
watching myself
and i'm afraid to move
“sorry”
watching you
watching me
you know i adore you, yes?
doom
here now and in my dreams too.
because i adore you
and i think about you
i have an idea
but only in the way i wish it could be
you should run away as fast as you can
go and don't look back

i remember the time
you lifted my shirt
looking up
you asked “is this okay?”
i winced because it was
and because no one ever asks for permission
and because it hasn't happened again
and because i didn't know i was in a moment i wouldn't forget
until the moment passed

i remember the look
that you gave me
you gave me much more than that
i remember asking for permission

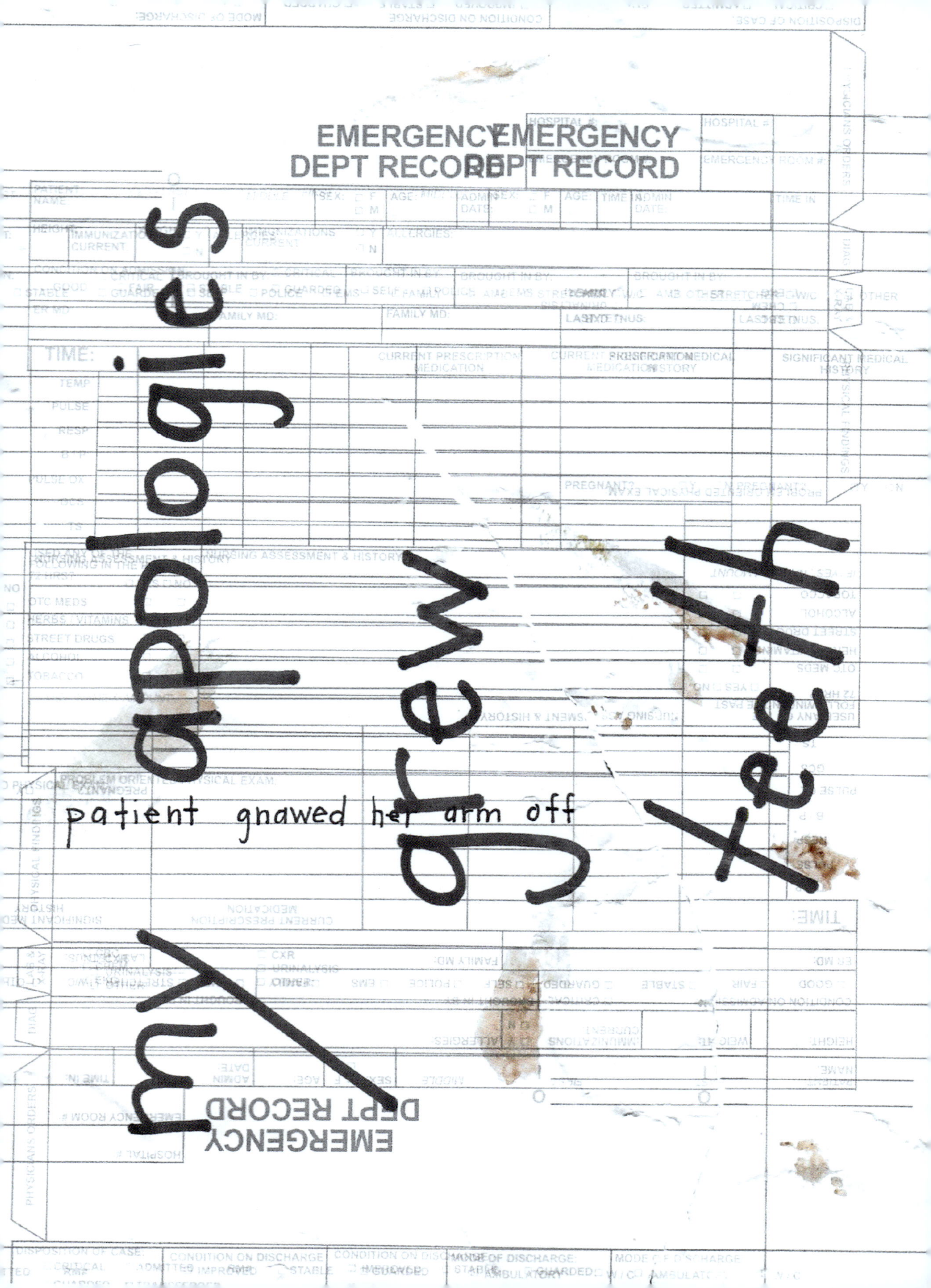
EMERGENCY DEPT RECORD
my apologies
grew
teeth
patient gnawed her arm off

made a muse
out of an enigma

Memo No.
Date / /

my toy soldier
stuck on the shelf
armed with only the ability to
gaze at love

and not step into it

CORDEI
2026

CORDEIRO
2026

God?
Karma?
“The greater good?”

Who is keeping score?

dear June,

“Rules” are an invention of convention.

in another universe we’re having the best sex of our lives,

A means of controlling the uncontrollable.

but in this universe

Conformity to animalistic tendencies.

Who the fuck wins in a game of rules?

you don’t chase and i’m too stubborn,

The rule makers.

and if you make me feel desperate for anything,

The writers of the Bible were the greatest sinners,

i’ll go without it twice as

Probably so disgusted with themselves, they projected their own morality in holy stories.

long

So yes, **All is fair in love & war.**

to spite myself

and you

And if you disagree, you’re probably just scared of yourself.

because fuck you
but i adore you •
and i want to fuck you
but also fuck you

theres a bullet hole where you kissed me

11. Surface Anatomy of the Upper Extremity

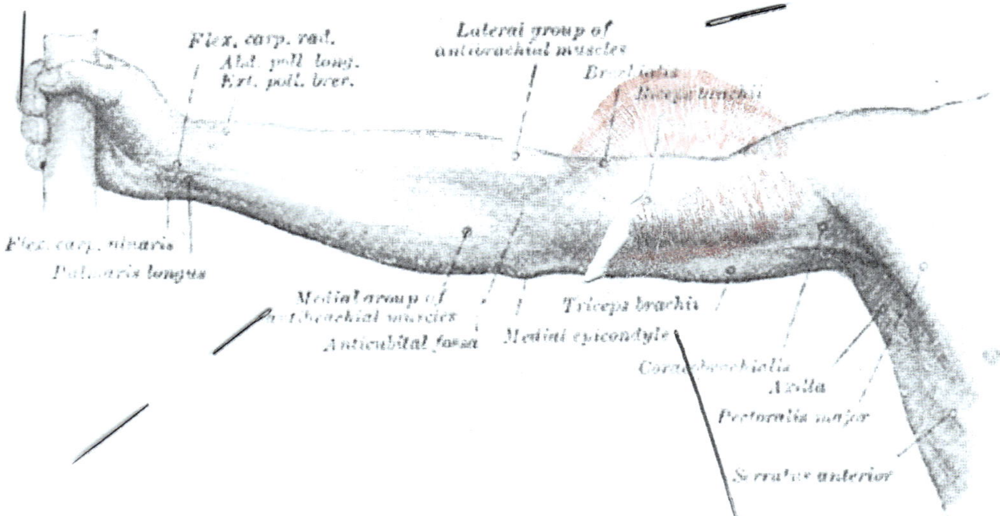

FIG. 1231– Front of right upper extremity.

the paper sighs at me

Fluttering
in clasped hands

Heartbeat
in your palms

Scared to kill a bird before it can fly
Scared to open your eyes

You want it to be saved

You think I'm waiting on   you?

No.

I'm cracking my knuckles
checking my shoulder
pacing and searching
the shadows

For a dead girl

maybe because the colors were
swirling together

and i was supposed to be scared
but i was *smiling*

for a second

i liked the way it felt

to be

pulled under

flower crowns

a tombstone

a lady wearing white

if you walked the graveyard to
find my name, you'd see the word:

Why?

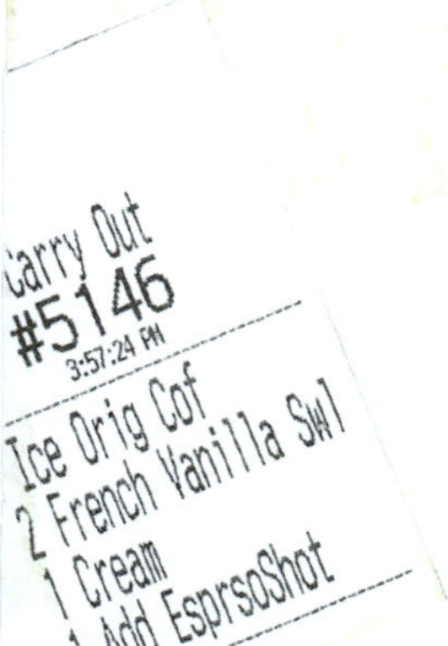

Memo No. [redacted]
Date [redacted]

You're there
and I'm here

but let the words I speak be
a bridge

You are not gone
You will never be gone
Because you are not gone

And I won't be jealous of angels anymore
And I won't be mad at God anymore
And I won't let the grey rot my bones

I will giggle and curtsy at the sky
I will wink at you in the dark
I will twirl in pieres of your legacy

And when I close my eyes,
I will follow you down the long hallways
of my dreams

Will you wear my ashes
in a heart shaped locket?

PLACE
STAMP
HERE

WHO IS GOD?

God is a bridge
in a POST CARD
that almost saw you jump

and the lighthouse below
that begged you to stay
sometimes I think God is just me on my death bed
so when I talk to God, I'm talking to myself

the one much older
much wiser
who found this lesson
and the lessons to come

maybe God isn't watching
maybe God is in you

I'm sensitive
my tears thread silver linings

Fist to my eye lids
[redacted]
a peek at the galaxy

I just want to see

God, I think I need a smoke break
& you're smiling because I dont even smoke

setting up a tea party in the
dark so we can all get well
acquainted.

come out
come out
wherever you are

curves and roundness reprimand the rabid dog
I look at my bones in shame

Can They See Right *Through* Me?

The *vitality*
of women
a lush garden of green
it breathes to me
it calls to me,

"stop holding onto your bones so tightly,
you know you can't take them with you
to heaven"

they beg me to eat
to enjoy
to dance
to be

Close the windows
open the door

there's a room at the end of the
hall way

Fetters singing

where i've kept her sick and starving

she screams and she screams

Please stop screaming
she screams so loud

Eyelids flutter like a mourning
dove

I feel my collarbones to make
sure she's still there

and I wait for the ringing to
stop

do i
cut off
the tongue
that's memorized
your name?

99. Three Short Drawers, Ogee Bracket Foot. Lid with Lip Mold. Pennsylvania. Drawers Suggest Tables of Same Region. Howard Reifsnyder.

I used to cross the street to avoid you. Now I stare at ceilings

Drawers with lips came in about 1700. The later simpler New England pine chests did not have lipped drawers. A bracket foot as good as this is very rare on chests. The plain bracket seen below is usual. The finer specimens when not carved, in Pennsylvania, are in walnut. Three end to end drawers are rare.

The origin and date of a chest may be hinted at in the hinge. Decorative hinges are an indicative of the Delaware valley. Pin hinges mean New England. Plain strap hinges mean late New England.

100. Bracket Foot, Two End-to-End Lipped Drawers. Pennsylvania Style. 18th Century. Mrs. Francis P. Garvan.

a penny for my wounds

two sides
of the same   truth

You

a martyr

~~a martyr~~

a muse

like a pigeon
i too
only start to fly

when there's something to
crash into

"you're not like most girls"

i'm not like most girls because i *am*
most girls

i am a mosaic of every girl i've
ever met

because to be like "most girls" is a
revolutionary act

is counter culture

is to love yourself but hate the girl
who reminds you the **most** of you
because *how dare you???*

oh, to be a girl!

that girl and i are practically the
same

yet invisibly competing in a losing
game

why wouldn't i want to be like most
girls?

have you ever been around girls?

and if you so desire to be the girl
who is not like most girls...

congratulations, you are exactly
like most girls

turned my world
technicolor

and
walked
away

Memo No. sobriety
Date 08 / 02 / 25

ghastly metamorphosis
a mirrorball becomes a wallflower

hands held in question marks
the ghost of who I was
the most sparkly thing at the party

She flutters
two dimples and a bitten lip
while I stand
at my public execution

"it's humiliating." I tell her

"I'm fucking humiliated," I scream

Breaking
my
teeth

vanity.

one day you'll be the buffalo

tell me dear,
you think you are your fare?
you think you are your body?

well the lions will eat that too
and then will the hyenas
and then will the birds
and then will the dirt

dressed for the slaughter
oh the world!
and its appetite

Your trigger finger
exhales
Waiting for bigger game

Resin kisses
Running at headl ights

Jaw locked
P upils blown

Dead doe

Buck m ounted on the wall

Sparks on dry birch
Thirsty
thinking about a girl you used to know

Oh,
honey
This is the part where they orchestrate

the screaming

Yes, the wildfire symphony

Ashes in the blonde and I'm *damned*
to burn in your lungs forever

Closed - eyed bounty hunter
Phantom chasing
You. Wanted for a Midwest tragedy

Racing dreams to wake the sun
The fastest girl I knew

Gone

fingertips on my
r i b c a g e
lighting me like a
m a t c h
DINING - COCKTAILS

[redacted] it aches a little more in the rain

the empty streets and shuffled feet
the puddles and their revelations

i never knew i'd know love
only after i knew you

I draw maps often
Delicate little verses

Just in case you wanted to find me
Just in case you're looking
Just in case

Ribbon tangled
Bitten by barbed wire
Boxing

barefoot in California

at least you know where
i started

and where i ended.

I remember your hands
on the precipice of my breasts
looking up
asking,
"Is this okay?"

I winced at the consideration
Sitting deeper
into the first lap
that's ever
asked
for permission

This
is the red in every poem I tried to paint

This is when I became a dog

Scratching

Please
Let
Me
In

howling
and
Draping myself
in places
I knew you'd be

Our closed mouths
"sorry, sorry"

Our hungry eyes
"we can't do this lightly"

Our consolation prize

This is the dirt I dug
looking for my own bones

This is the wound you hold
in your hands

And this is the confession:

There was a time I thought I'd always keep
a hole in the fence for you

That if you ever came back
I'd be there

Tail wagging

Waiting

to bury the bird

like a lucky penny on cracked
pavement

finding silver linings is my
specialty

the best part of being let go
is now

I'm free

COMPLIMENTS OF BOSTON SUNDAY AMERICAN

POST-CARD

POSTAGE:
1c. for United States and Canada;
2c. for abroad.

M I've got to get the dirt

out of my

fingernails

THIS SIDE IS EXCLUSIVELY FOR THE ADDRESS

75

Darling,
Go on

Tell us about the night sky
when your gulps were ecstasy
How they said you'd feel love
and you felt alone

Nameless and championed
Responsible for no one
the rover's journey

Tell us about that.

The man in the Kitchen
finding a lighter
nipping at your belt loops

an unfed beast
leashed

your hair was long then
Go on,
we remember

A sip of sour water
free

you used to hate me, *how I ruined your party*

Look at the scatter sweet girl
that means it's morning
that means you are being saved

You
with a lover,
a child calling you "Mom"

Your porch, swinging
when everyone is dead

you used to hate me, You, the same girl they call
the Sun

Your wrinkled hands, your bluest eyes
wearing the loss

Sweet girl, engulfed in yellow,
you're formless, squirming
and so scared of a God

ONE DAY i WILL
HAVE KISSED EVERY
SQUARE INCH OF
YOUR BODY.

immortalized by devotion
the metamorphosis of love

veiled swans
shattered glass
knelt
washing my feet

my spirit blossoms in your
shadow
my body Kaleidoscopes in
your light

Romances spoken dance along the cosmos
found again and again and again

The fastest way to die
is to hold a confession in your throat

Spoken love creates
life and opens portals

The audacity of love and its ability
to change Everything

The tongue is a tool of fate

I survive
I plunge

into the depths

Let my legacy be measured in tears

Let the life that flashes before my eyes
Be when you saw me naked for the
First Time

And in heaven when they ask if I have
any regrets
Let it be that I didn't jump off more
bridges
To Kiss more fishes

So when I arrive
soaking wet
and freshly Kissed

They will already Know my name

Thank You!

as **much** as this book is about heartbreak, it only exists because of love.

to Nick, who has summoned the most beautiful parts of me to the surface, this book is only born from your influence, meeting you _is_ the best thing that's ever happened to me. you are everything i've ever longed and searched for, i love you SO much,

to my parents who gave me the greatest gift of all — a chance to exist in this human body and experience life!!! my two favorite people, I love you so much.

to my siblings, the closest thing I know to home, who know our own lived story so intimately... i will never feel alone,

to Daniel, my publisher, for taking a chance on a girl with a submission of handwritten scanned poems, who insisted on the artistic integrity and soul of this book, thank you for bringing this book to fruition, I'm so lucky,

to Janaka, my creative midwife, for enriching and guiding me to and through the birth of *Whiskers of a Kitten*,

to Gabi, my love for your philosophy is and was my yellow brick road, your guidance and generosity has imprinted me forever,

to Ian's cover design and Haley's dream, this cover encapsulates both womanhood and girlhood, innocence and wisdom, thank you,

to my family and friends who believe in me and hold me up right, who see me so clearly, thank you, ♡

to New York City, your potency is intoxicating you are life force, the catalyst of my artistry, and a place i can finally call home,

to the most tender of heartbreakers,
ex lovers, one night stands and friends
I kissed,

for every moment, no matter how fleeting
that I believed in love and felt
ALIVE was worth it,

to the innocence lost,
the wisdom gained
in pursuit of LOVE and LIFE,

I'd do it all again and learn it twice.

thank you.